GROSS FOODS

Pete Jenkins

Rourke
Educational Media

rourkeeducationalmedia.com

Guided Reading Level: **P**

Scan for Related Titles and Teacher Resources

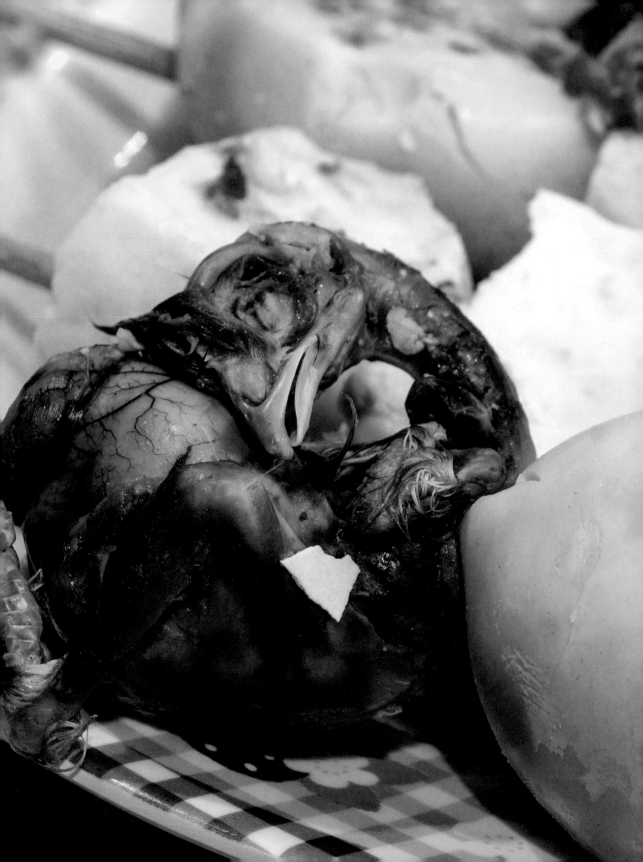

TABLE OF CONTENTS

Maggot cheese, Mongolian Boodog, soft-boiled fetal duck. When it comes to gross foods, the world is full of it.

But the question is, who eats this stuff?

YOU WANT ME TO

Vital organs of just about every species have been eaten at one time or another. Hoofs, beaks, ears, and eyeballs have all been served up on a plate.

Marmots inflate as they cook and can get as big as a basketball with four little legs sticking out. It might even explode right in your lap.

4

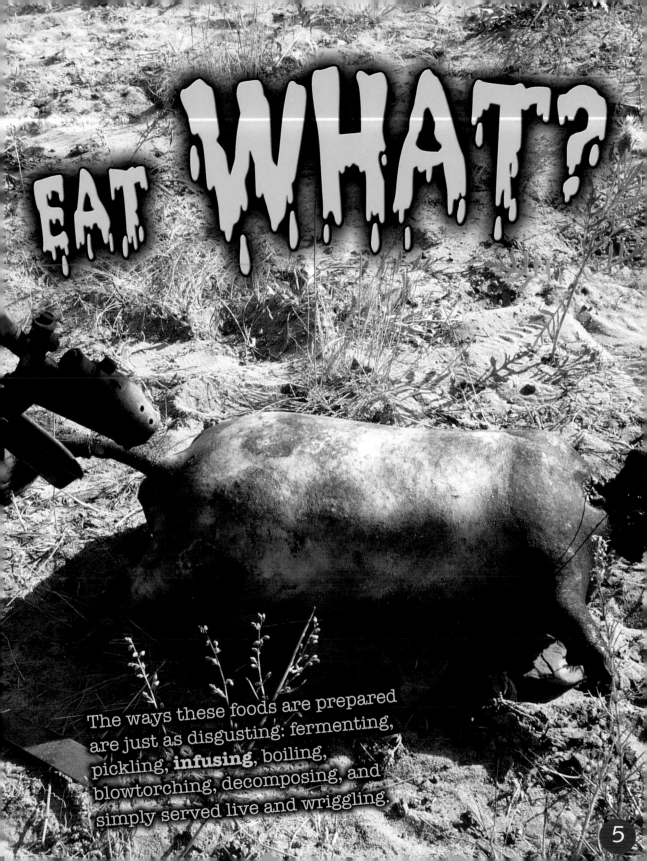

EAT WHAT?

The ways these foods are prepared are just as disgusting: fermenting, pickling, **infusing**, boiling, blowtorching, decomposing, and simply served live and wriggling.

People around the world eat some dishes that you might not consider touching in a million years. But, as disgusting as they are, many have deep cultural roots. Some are common side dishes of famous feasts and served on the tables of kings.

Puffins are tiny, cute little birds. But can you imagine eating the heart of one? They are considered a delicacy in Iceland.

Rocky Mountain oysters don't actually contain oysters at all. They are deep fried testicles of young bulls.

GAG-SEEKERS

Many culinary adventurers may find these foods exciting to try, but most people would politely say, "No, thank you!"

Let's dive right in to some of these gastric delights—or should we say frights?

Balut takes the grossest spot in the egg category. These are fertilized duck eggs, allowed to grow for a certain period of time. People then peel back the shell to feast on not only a soft boiled egg, but also the body of a fetal duck. Bones, feathers, beak and all. Balut fans suggest slurping it right from the shell with a pinch of salt.

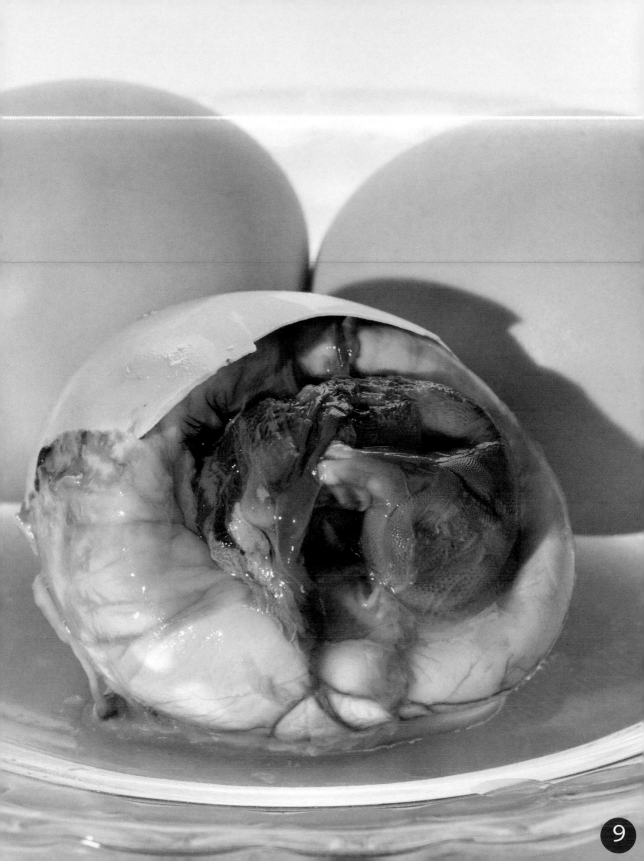

But wait, it gets even better. Ever thought about having sheep's head for your school lunch?

Sheep's head is a traditional **delicacy** served in a number of world regions, including the Mediterranean and Northern Europe.

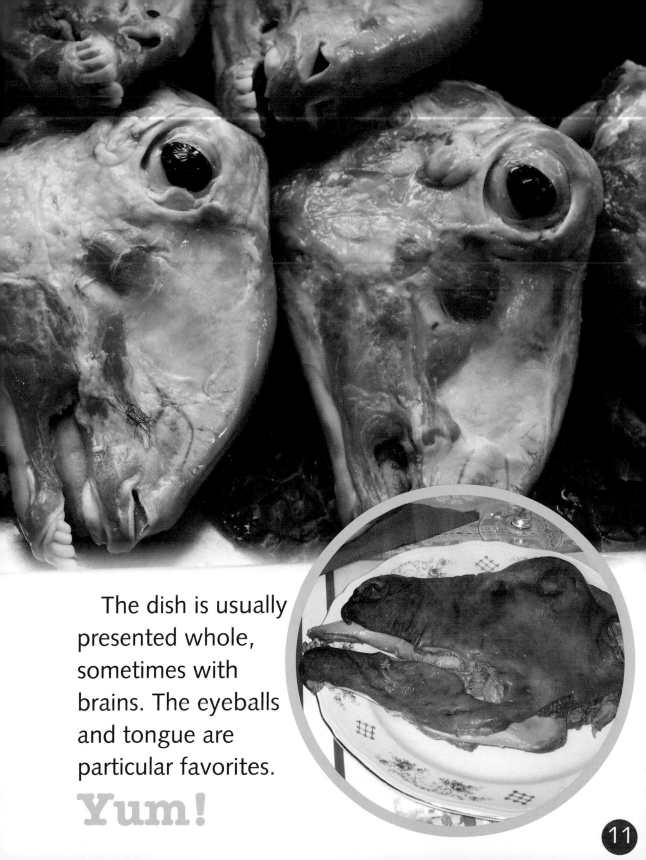

The dish is usually presented whole, sometimes with brains. The eyeballs and tongue are particular favorites. **Yum!**

Casu Marzu, also called maggot cheese, is a pecorino cheese and a Sardinian delicacy. Although steeped in Italian history, it is so disgusting it is illegal to sell.

It is prepared by leaving the cheese outside where flies lay their **larvae** all over it, which eventually turn into fat, juicy maggots. After this **fermentation** process is complete, voila! It's ready to eat.

This cheese tastes exactly as you might imagine: strong pecorino, with the crawly, snot-plump bodies of insect larvae, and the slimy fat they've made of the digested cheese. Oh, and the maggots jump off the cheese while you're eating it!

FOODS THAT MAKE

YOU PUKE

Raw foods are not uncommon in Asian **cuisine**. But what if it is still alive and squirming all over your plate? A baby octopus, also called **sannakji**, may be served cut into bite-sized, still-wriggling pieces, suction cups and all.

People also slurp this squirming sea creature whole. As you might imagine the octopus is rubbery, chewy, and fairly tasteless. Some brave foodies say the suction cups may stick in your mouth on the way down.

Cambodians have hunted spiders for medicine and food for generations, but eating them became widespread in the mid-1970s. Thai zebra tarantulas, called apin, are about the size of your palm.

Female spiders are sought after because the eggs they carry are considered especially flavorful.

The most popular way to cook these creepy crawlers is to season them with soy sauce, garlic, salt, and sugar, and fry them until crispy. The body, which has the most meat, is said to be the best part of the spider.

Alaska is known for salmon, but have you ever heard of stink head? It's not the traditional way to cook this tasty fish. Not even close.

In this mouth-watering recipe, the heads of the salmon are cut off, wrapped in plastic and put in fermentation pits to rot and **decompose** for a few weeks.

After the fermentation process is complete, the heads are then harvested and served as a putty-like mash.

Yum! Pass the chips, please!

KILLER FOODS

Everyone enjoys a good cookie now and then. What's your favorite kind? Oatmeal, maybe peanut butter, or maybe a nice wasp cookie. Yep, you heard it right!

In Japan, they make these delectable cookies just like you would a chocolate chip cookie, but the wasps replace the chips. They are made with digger wasps, which are known to cause a pretty bad sting. Good luck to your tongue!

According to some sources, wasps contain the highest percentage of protein of any edible insect—a whopping 81 percent to be exact! The average steak contains just 20 percent.

In Mexico, Escamoles, also known as insect caviar, is made from the larvae and pupae of ants that are harvested from the mescal or tequila plant.

Considered to be a delicacy, it is said to have a nutty, buttery taste with the consistency of cottage cheese. Pass the plate, please!

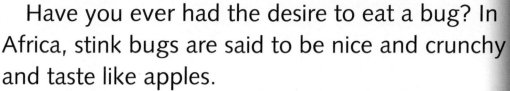

Have you ever had the desire to eat a bug? In Africa, stink bugs are said to be nice and crunchy and taste like apples.

They can also be used in soups or stews. When they are boiled, they release a defensive pheromone, or odor, in a last attempt to survive. The scent hurts your eyes, similar to what happens when you peel an onion and it makes you cry.

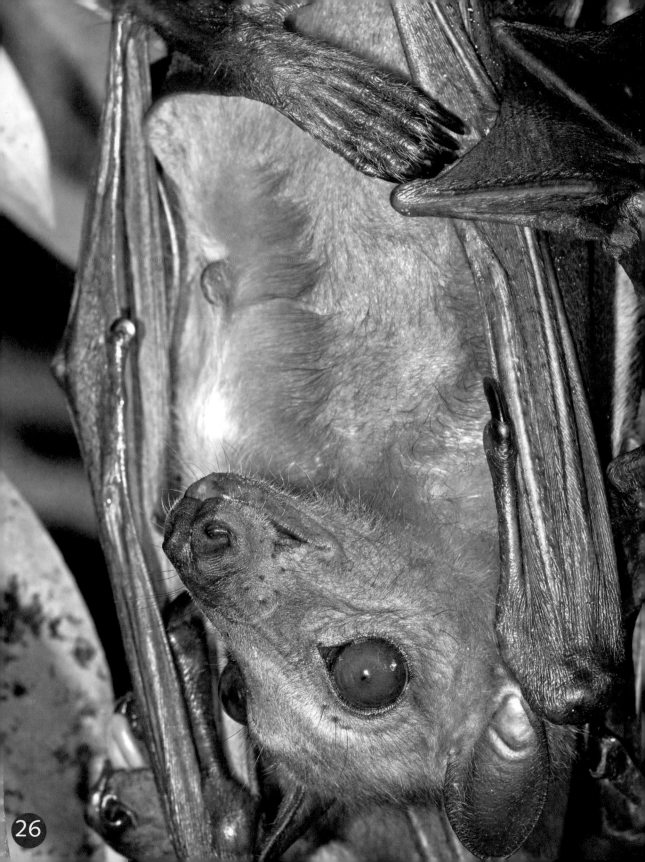

Have you ever sat down for a dinner featuring fruit-bat soup? Yeah, I didn't think so. Bats are part of the native cuisine in Thailand, Guam, and parts of China.

Just wash up a few bats, season them with ginger onion and plop them in some water. Oh, one more thing. Bats are known to carry an **abundance** of diseases, so be careful or this could be your last meal.

If soup isn't your thing, you could always make bat **paste**. Just boil the flying critters and then chop them into a mash or paste. Warning: Don't brush your teeth with it!

All over the world people eat some pretty strange things. To them they may seem quite normal. Who knows, maybe they think the things we eat are just as weird.

Somehow, I don't think so. Bugs, brains, maggots? All I can say is,

GROSS ME

fried silkworms   scorpion kabobs

OUT!

crickets
on sticks

GLOSSARY

abundance (uh-BUHN-duhns): to have a wide availability or present in great quantities

cuisine (kwi-ZEEN): a style or manner of presenting or cooking food

decompose (dee-kuhm-POZE): to rot or decay

delicacy (del-ik-uh-SEE): a food item that is considered highly desired

fermentation (fur-MENT-a-shuhn): when the sugars in a liquid turn into alchohol

infusing (in-FYOOZ-een): to soak in a liquid to extract flavor or healing properties

larvae (LAHR-vee): insects at the stage of development between an egg and a pupa

paste (payst): a soft, creamy mixture made by mashing food until smooth

sannakji (SAN-ahk-jee): a variety of hoe, or raw fish, in Asian cuisine

vital (VYE-tuhl): very important or essential

INDEX

SHOW WHAT YOU KNOW

1. Why can bats be dangerous to eat?
2. In what part of the world are stink bugs eaten?
3. Would you ever be brave enough to try one of these foods? Why or why not?
4. In what area of the world are raw food items consumed?
5. When eating fried spiders, why are the females considered to be better?

WEBSITES TO VISIT

www.hostelworld.com/blog/the-50-weirdest-foods-from-around-the-world/158695

www.roughguides.com/gallery/weird-food/#/0

www.toptenz.net/top-ten-grossest-foods.php

About the Author

Pete Jenkins has traveled quite a bit during his life. Although he has tried some foods he wasn't crazy about, he was never crazy enough to try any of the foods in this book. He will take a cheeseburger and fries, please!

Meet The Author!
www.meetREMauthors.com

www.rourkeeducationalmedia.com

PHOTO CREDITS: Cover: bug bkground © John David Bigl III, girl © Kamira, duck egg © Rangzen, fly larvae © AijaK all from Shutterstock. Pages 2-3 © 9george Shutterstock; Pages 4-5 © Bogomolov.PL; pages 6-7 puffins © Hartmut Albert Shutterstock, page 7 rocky mountain oysters © Sklathill at http://flickr.com/photos/70857039@N00/119083080 , young bulls © RussieseO Shutterstock; pages 8-9 © Seanjeeves | Dreamstime.com; pages 10-11 © simonox Shutterstock, inset photo © PerPlex; page 12-13 Casu Marzu © Shardan https://creativecommons.org/licenses/by-sa/2.5/deed.en , flies and larva © Sergey Goruppa Shutterstock, maggots © valeriiaarnaud Shutterstock; pages 14-15 © successo images Shutterstock; pages 16-17 © Peter Stuckings Shutterstock, inset photo page 17 © Sviluppo-Shutterstock; pages 18-19 © Junpinzon Dreamstime, page 18 inset photo © Hsagencia Dreamstime; page 20 © paulrommer Shutterstock, page 21 © Kamira Shutterstock; pages 22-23 © GETSARAPORN Shutterstock, inset photo page 23 © Cvmontuy; page 24 boy © Celig, bug © Pan Xunbin both Shutterstock, page 25 © dragi52 Shutterstock; page 27 © davemhuntphotography, page 27 soup © mattjlc at http_flickr.com_photos_23457733@N05_3638131737 ; page 28-29 GROSS ME OUT! letters © Cory Thoman, scorpions © Anastasiia Konsta, fried silkworms © Anastasiia Konsta, crickets © D. Kucharski K. Kucharska, page 29 girl © Kamira all from Shutterstock

Edited by: Keli Sipperley

Cover and Interior design by: Nicola Stratford   www.nicolastratford.com

Library of Congress PCN Data

Gross Foods / Pete Jenkins
(Gross Me Out!)
 ISBN 978-1-68191-768-9 (hard cover)
 ISBN 978-1-68191-869-3 (soft cover)
 ISBN 978-1-68191-957-7 (e-Book)
Library of Congress Control Number: 2016932728

Rourke Educational Media
Printed in the United States of America, North Mankato, Minnesota

Also Available as:

ROURKE'S
e-Books